The Ultimate Guide to Starting Your Own Virtual Assistant Business

Neil King

Table Of Contents

Introduction

Why start a virtual assistant business?

Why start a virtual assistant business?

There are countless reasons why starting a virtual assistant business could be the best decision you ever make. For starters, the demand for virtual assistants is on the rise, as more businesses and entrepreneurs look to outsource their administrative tasks and focus on their core competencies. This means that there is a growing market for your services, and plenty of opportunities to build a thriving business.

But the benefits of starting a virtual assistant business go beyond just financial gain. As a virtual assistant, you have the freedom to work from anywhere, at any time, and on your own terms. You can choose the clients you work with, the tasks you take on, and the hours you work. This level of flexibility is perfect for anyone looking for a side hustle, or for those who want to build a business that fits around their lifestyle.

Another reason to start a virtual assistant business is the variety of services you can offer. From social media management and email marketing to website design and administrative support, there are countless ways to add value to your clients' businesses. This means that you can choose the services that you enjoy the most, and that align with your skills and interests.

One of the most rewarding aspects of starting a virtual assistant business is the opportunity to help others. As a virtual assistant, you will be providing valuable support to entrepreneurs and businesses who need it most. By taking on their administrative tasks, you are freeing up their time and energy to focus on what they do best. This can be incredibly fulfilling, and can lead to long-lasting relationships with your clients.

In summary, starting a virtual assistant business is a smart choice for anyone looking to build a flexible, rewarding business that aligns with their skills and interests. With a growing market for your services, a wide range of services to offer, and the ability to help others, there has never been a better time to start your own virtual assistant business.

Who can start a virtual assistant business?

Who Can Start a Virtual Assistant Business?

The answer to this question is simple – anyone can start a virtual assistant business. Whether you are a stay-at-home mom, a recent college graduate, a retiree, or anyone who is interested in starting a side hustle, a virtual assistant business is a great option for you.

One of the best things about starting a virtual assistant business is that you don't need any special qualifications or experience. You don't need a degree in business or marketing, and you don't need to have worked in an office before. All you need is a computer, internet connection, and the willingness to learn.

Virtual assistant businesses can be started by anyone with a passion for helping others and a desire to work from home. If you have experience in any of the niches mentioned above, that's even better. You can offer your services in these areas and become a specialist in your field.

Social media management, email marketing, website design and development, administrative support, and content creation are all services that businesses need. By offering these services as a virtual assistant, you can help busy entrepreneurs and small business owners grow their businesses while earning a living from home.

Additionally, virtual assistant businesses are not limited by location. You can work with clients from all over the world, which means that your potential client base is limitless. With the rise of technology, it has become easier than ever to work remotely and connect with clients online.

In conclusion, anyone can start a virtual assistant business. You don't need any special qualifications or experience – just a computer, internet connection, and a willingness to learn. By offering valuable services to businesses, you can help them grow while building a successful and fulfilling career from home.

What skills do you need to start a virtual assistant business?

Starting your own virtual assistant business can be an excellent way to earn a living and work from home. It can also be a great side hustle for those who want to earn extra income while maintaining a full-time job. However, starting a virtual assistant business requires specific skills that are essential for success in this field.

One of the most important skills you need as a virtual assistant is excellent communication skills. As a virtual assistant, you will be communicating with clients through various channels, such as email, phone, or video conferencing. You should be able to communicate clearly, professionally, and effectively, and understand your clients' needs and requirements.

Another essential skill for a virtual assistant is time management. You will be working on multiple tasks and projects simultaneously, and you need to be able to prioritize and manage your time effectively to meet deadlines. You should also be able to work independently and be self-motivated to stay focused on tasks and complete them on time.

As a virtual assistant, you should also have excellent computer skills and be proficient in using various software and online tools. You should be comfortable with using social media platforms, email marketing tools, website builders, and other software relevant to your niche.

Depending on your niche, you may also need specific skills such as website design and development, content creation and copywriting, administrative support, or social media management. It's essential to invest time and effort into learning these skills and staying up-to-date with the latest trends and technologies in your niche.

In conclusion, starting a virtual assistant business requires a combination of skills, including excellent communication skills, time management, computer proficiency, and niche-specific skills. By developing and honing these skills, you can build a successful virtual assistant business and achieve your goals.

What you can expect from this book?

What You Can Expect from This Book?

Welcome to the Ultimate Guide to Starting Your Own Virtual Assistant Business. This book is written for anyone who wants to start a successful virtual assistant business or side hustle. Whether you are a stay-at-home mom, a college student, or anyone who wants to work from home, this book is for you.

In this book, you will learn step-by-step how to start and run a successful virtual assistant business. You will discover the tools, techniques, and strategies that you need to succeed in this industry. You will learn how to find clients, market your services, and deliver exceptional results.

The virtual assistant industry is growing rapidly, and there is a high demand for skilled professionals who can provide quality services to businesses of all sizes. This means that there is a huge opportunity for you to start your own virtual assistant business and earn a good income.

In this book, you will learn how to:

- Set up your virtual assistant business

- Choose a niche that suits your skills and interests

- Find clients and market your services

- Set your prices and manage your finances

- Provide exceptional customer service

- Manage your time and work effectively

- Grow your business and expand your services

This book covers a range of niches within the virtual assistant industry, including social media management, email marketing, website design and development, administrative support, content creation, and copywriting. You will learn how to provide these services to your clients and become an expert in your niche.

By the end of this book, you will have the knowledge, skills, and confidence to start and run your own successful virtual assistant business. You will be able to work from home, choose your own hours, and enjoy the freedom and flexibility that comes with being your own boss.

So if you are ready to start your own virtual assistant business, grab a copy of this book and get started today!

Starting Your Virtual Assistant Business

The Ultimate Guide to Starting Your Own Virtual Assistant Business

Is starting a virtual assistant business right for you?

Is starting a virtual assistant business right for you? This is a question that many aspiring entrepreneurs ask themselves before diving into the world of virtual assistance. The answer is not always straightforward, as it depends on various factors such as your skills, experience, and willingness to learn and adapt.

Firstly, it is essential to consider your strengths and weaknesses. Are you an excellent communicator, organized, and able to multitask efficiently? Do you have experience in administrative support, social media management, email marketing, website design and development, or content creation and copywriting? If you have a strong skill set in any of these areas, you may be well-suited to start a virtual assistant business.

Additionally, it is crucial to have the right mindset and attitude towards entrepreneurship. Starting a virtual assistant business requires a lot of hard work, dedication, and perseverance. You need to be willing to put in the effort to build your business from scratch, network with potential clients, and continually learn and improve your skills.

Another factor to consider is your financial situation. Starting a virtual assistant business may require some initial investment in tools and resources such as a website, software, and training courses. It is important to have a realistic budget and a plan for how you will finance your business in the early stages.

If you have weighed the pros and cons and are confident that starting a virtual assistant business is right for you, the next step is to determine your niche. Are you interested in providing social media management, email marketing services, website design and development, administrative support, or content creation and copywriting? It is essential to choose a niche that aligns with your strengths and interests and has a high demand in the market.

In conclusion, starting a virtual assistant business can be a rewarding and fulfilling venture for those with the right skills, mindset, and financial situation. However, it is essential to weigh the pros and cons and determine if it is the right fit for you before taking the plunge.

Creating a business plan for your virtual assistant business

Creating a Business Plan for Your Virtual Assistant Business

Starting a virtual assistant business is exciting, but it can also be overwhelming. Like any business, it requires careful planning and strategizing to ensure its success. Developing a business plan can help you define your goals, identify your target market, and plan your finances. Here are some steps to create a business plan for your virtual assistant business.

Identify Your Goals

Your business plan should begin with a clear statement of your goals. What do you hope to accomplish with your virtual assistant business? Do you want to work full-time or part-time? Do you want to specialize in a particular niche, such as social media management or website design? Defining your goals will help you focus your efforts and measure your success.

Determine Your Target Market

Identifying your target market is essential to the success of your virtual assistant business. Who are your ideal clients? What industries do they work in? What are their pain points and needs? Understanding your target market will help you tailor your services and marketing efforts to attract and retain clients.

Plan Your Finances

Starting a virtual assistant business requires some upfront investment. You'll need to invest in equipment, software, and marketing materials. Determine your startup costs and ongoing expenses, such as website hosting and software subscriptions. Create a budget and determine how much you need to charge for your services to cover your expenses and make a profit.

Marketing Strategy

Create a marketing strategy that will help you reach your target market. Consider social media marketing, email marketing, and networking events. You can also offer free consultations and workshops to attract potential clients.

Conclusion

Creating a business plan is a critical step in starting a virtual assistant business. It will help you define your goals, identify your target market, plan your finances, and develop a marketing strategy. With a solid business plan in place, you'll be better prepared to launch and grow your virtual assistant business.

Setting up your home office

Setting up your home office is an important task for anyone starting their own virtual assistant business. Your home office is where you will be spending most of your time, and it is important to create a space that is comfortable and conducive to productivity.

The first step in setting up your home office is to choose a dedicated space. This space should be quiet and free from interruptions. It should also be large enough to accommodate your desk, chair, and any other equipment you may need, such as a printer or scanner.

Once you have chosen your space, you need to consider your equipment. The most important piece of equipment for a virtual assistant is a computer, so it is essential to choose a high-quality device that can handle the demands of your work. You may also need a printer, scanner, and other peripherals, depending on the services you offer.

In addition to your equipment, you will also need to consider your furniture. Your desk and chair should be comfortable and ergonomic to prevent any pain or discomfort during long hours of work. You may also want to consider adding additional storage, such as shelves or filing cabinets, to keep your workspace organized and clutter-free.

Finally, you need to consider your lighting and decor. Good lighting is essential for productivity, so choose a space with plenty of natural light or invest in a good desk lamp. Decor can also have a big impact on your mood and productivity, so choose colors and decor that inspire and motivate you.

In conclusion, setting up your home office is an essential step in starting your own virtual assistant business. By choosing a dedicated space, investing in high-quality equipment and furniture, and considering your lighting and decor, you can create a space that is comfortable, productive, and conducive to success.

Choosing your niche and services

Choosing your niche and services is a crucial step when starting your own virtual assistant business. This decision will determine the type of clients you attract, the services you offer, and ultimately, the success of your business. In this subchapter, we will discuss the different niches and services that you can offer as a virtual assistant, and how to choose the right one for you.

Virtual Assistant Business:

If you have a diverse skill set and enjoy assisting with a variety of tasks, then a general virtual assistant business may be the perfect niche for you. You can offer services such as administrative support, email management, scheduling, and social media management. This niche is perfect for those who are just starting out and want to gain experience in different areas.

Social Media Management:

With the rise of social media platforms, many businesses are in need of social media management services. If you have a passion for social media and enjoy creating engaging content, then this niche may be the perfect fit for you. You can offer services such as content creation, social media strategy, and community management.

Email Marketing Services:

Email marketing is a powerful tool for businesses to promote their products and services. If you have experience with email marketing software and enjoy creating engaging email campaigns, then this niche may be the perfect fit for you. You can offer services such as email campaign creation, list management, and email automation.

Website Design and Development:

If you have experience with website design and development, then this niche may be the perfect fit for you. You can offer services such as website design, website development, and website maintenance. This niche is perfect for those who have a creative eye and enjoy working with websites.

Administrative Support:

Administrative support is a necessary function for many businesses. If you have experience with administrative tasks such as data entry, scheduling, and email management, then this niche may be the perfect fit for you. You can offer services such as administrative support, customer service, and project management.

Content Creation and Copywriting:

If you have a passion for writing and enjoy creating engaging content, then this niche may be the perfect fit for you. You can offer services such as blog post creation, article writing, and copywriting. This niche is perfect for those who have a creative writing style and enjoy working with words.

In conclusion, when choosing your niche and services, it's important to consider your skills, interests, and experience. By choosing a niche that aligns with your strengths, you'll be able to offer high-quality services and attract the right clients. Remember to also consider the demand for your niche and the competition in the market. With the right niche and services, you'll be able to build a successful virtual assistant business.

Setting your prices and rates

Setting your prices and rates is one of the most important decisions you will make when starting your own virtual assistant business. Pricing can be tricky, but it is crucial to set a rate that is fair to you and your clients. Here are some tips to help you set your prices and rates:

1. Research your competitors: Before setting your rates, research what other virtual assistants in your niche are charging. This will give you an idea of what the market is willing to pay and help you set competitive rates.

2. Determine your hourly rate: You need to determine your hourly rate based on your expenses, the amount of time you plan to work each week, and the income you want to generate. Calculate your hourly rate by dividing your desired annual income by the number of billable hours you plan to work each year.

3. Consider project-based pricing: Some clients prefer project-based pricing instead of hourly rates. This means that you will charge a flat fee for a specific project. Make sure to factor in your time, expenses, and the scope of the project when determining your project-based pricing.

4. Offer package deals: Offering package deals can be a great way to attract clients and generate more income. Consider offering a bundle of services at a discounted rate to incentivize clients to work with you.

5. Don't undervalue your services: It can be tempting to set low rates to attract clients, but this can hurt your business in the long run. Make sure to charge a rate that is fair to you and reflects the value of your services.

Setting your prices and rates can be a challenging task, but it is crucial to your success as a virtual assistant. By researching your competitors, determining your hourly rate, considering project-based pricing, offering package deals, and not undervaluing your services, you can set rates that are fair to you and your clients.

Building your brand and online presence

Building Your Brand and Online Presence

In today's digital age, having a strong online presence and brand identity is crucial for any business, including virtual assistant businesses. Your brand and online presence are what sets you apart from your competitors and makes you memorable to potential clients. Here are some tips to help you build your brand and online presence:

1. Define your brand: Before you start building your brand, you need to define what it is. Your brand is more than just a logo or tagline. It's the overall perception that people have of your business. To define your brand, think about your values, mission, and unique selling proposition. What sets you apart from other virtual assistant businesses?

2. Create a website: Your website is the foundation of your online presence. It's where potential clients will go to learn more about your business and services. Make sure your website is professional, easy to navigate, and reflects your brand identity.

3. Develop a social media strategy: Social media is a powerful tool for building your online presence and connecting with potential clients. Develop a social media strategy that aligns with your brand and business goals. Consider which platforms your target audience uses and create engaging content that showcases your expertise.

4. Offer email marketing services: Email marketing is a great way to stay in touch with your clients and keep them informed about your services. Offer email marketing services as part of your virtual assistant business. Use email marketing to promote your services, share industry news and trends, and provide valuable content to your subscribers.

5. Provide quality administrative support: As a virtual assistant, administrative support is at the core of your business. Make sure you provide quality administrative support that reflects your brand and business values. Be responsive, reliable, and professional in all your interactions with clients.

6. Create engaging content: Content creation and copywriting are essential for building your online presence and establishing yourself as an expert in your field. Create engaging content that showcases your expertise and provides value to your target audience. Use content to educate, inspire, and engage potential clients.

In conclusion, building your brand and online presence is essential for success in the virtual assistant business. Define your brand, create a professional website, develop a social media strategy, offer email marketing services, provide quality administrative support, and create engaging content. By following these tips, you'll be on your way to building a strong brand and online presence that sets you apart from your competitors.

Social Media Management for Virtual Assistant Businesses

The importance of social media for virtual assistant businesses

In today's digital age, social media has become an essential component of any successful business. This is especially true for virtual assistant businesses, which rely heavily on online channels to reach and engage with clients. In this subchapter, we'll explore why social media is important for virtual assistant businesses and how you can leverage it to grow your business.

First and foremost, social media provides a cost-effective way to market your virtual assistant business. By creating profiles on popular platforms like Facebook, Instagram, and Twitter, you can reach a large audience of potential clients without spending a dime on advertising. Social media also allows you to target specific demographics and interests, making it easier to attract clients who are most likely to benefit from your services.

Another key benefit of social media for virtual assistant businesses is that it helps build trust and credibility with clients. By regularly posting informative and helpful content, you can position yourself as an expert in your field and demonstrate your value to potential clients. Additionally, social media provides a platform for clients to leave reviews and testimonials, which can be a powerful tool for attracting new business.

Social media also enables virtual assistant businesses to provide excellent customer service and support. By responding promptly to client inquiries and concerns on social media, you can build strong relationships with clients and create a positive reputation for your business. This can lead to repeat business and referrals, which are essential for long-term success.

In order to effectively leverage social media for your virtual assistant business, it's important to have a solid strategy in place. This may include creating a content calendar, engaging with followers and other industry professionals, and tracking key metrics to measure your success. By taking a strategic approach to social media, you can maximize its potential to grow your business and achieve your goals.

In conclusion, social media is a critical component of any successful virtual assistant business. By utilizing its many benefits, you can market your business, build trust and credibility with clients, provide excellent customer service, and ultimately grow your business to new heights.

How to create a social media strategy for your clients

Social media is an essential tool for businesses of all sizes and industries. It allows them to connect with their target audience, promote their products and services, and build brand awareness. As a virtual assistant, it's crucial to offer social media management as a service to your clients. However, before you dive into managing their social media accounts, you need to create a social media strategy.

A social media strategy is a plan that outlines how your clients' social media accounts will be managed and what goals they want to achieve. Here are some steps you can follow to create a social media strategy for your clients:

1. Determine your client's target audience: Understanding your client's target audience is essential to creating a successful social media strategy. You need to know who they are, what they like, and what kind of content they engage with.

2. Choose the right social media platforms: Not all social media platforms are created equal. Depending on your client's industry and target audience, some platforms may be more effective than others. For example, if your client is targeting millennials, you might want to focus on Instagram and TikTok.

3. Set realistic goals: Your clients should have specific goals they want to achieve through their social media accounts. These goals could be increasing brand awareness, driving website traffic, or generating leads. Make sure these goals are realistic and measurable.

4. Create a content calendar: A content calendar is a schedule of what content will be posted on your client's social media accounts and when. This should include a mix of promotional and educational content, as well as curated content from other sources.

5. Monitor and analyze performance: It's essential to track your client's social media performance to see what's working and what's not. Use analytics tools to measure metrics such as engagement, reach, and conversions.

Creating a social media strategy for your clients is a vital part of social media management. By following these steps, you can help your clients achieve their social media goals and grow their business.

How to manage social media accounts for your clients

Social media has become an integral part of any business's marketing strategy. However, managing social media accounts can be time-consuming and overwhelming for many small business owners. As a virtual assistant, offering social media management services can be a lucrative niche for your business. Here are some tips on how to manage social media accounts for your clients:

1. Understand your client's target audience: Before creating any social media content, it's important to understand your client's target audience. This will help you create content that resonates with their followers and helps to grow their audience.

2. Develop a content strategy: Creating a content strategy is important to ensure that your client's social media accounts are consistently updated with fresh and engaging content. This may include posting a mix of promotional posts, educational posts, and engaging posts.

3. Use a social media management tool: There are many social media management tools available that can help you schedule and publish content across various social media platforms. These tools can also help you track analytics and engagement for your client's social media accounts.

4. Engage with followers: Social media isn't just about posting content; it's also about engaging with followers. Responding to comments and messages helps to build relationships with followers and can lead to increased engagement and sales for your client's business.

5. Stay up to date on social media trends: Social media is constantly evolving, and it's important to stay up to date on the latest trends and changes. This will help you create content that is relevant and engaging for your client's followers.

Offering social media management services can be a great way to grow your virtual assistant business. By understanding your client's target audience, developing a content strategy, using a social media management tool, engaging with followers, and staying up to date on social media trends, you can help your clients grow their social media presence and ultimately their business.

Tools and resources for social media management

Social media has become an essential aspect of businesses today. Social media management is a crucial aspect of any virtual assistant business that wants to stay ahead of the curve and help their clients achieve their goals. This subchapter will look at the tools and resources that can help manage social media effectively.

One of the most popular social media management tools is Hootsuite. It is a comprehensive tool that allows you to manage multiple social media accounts from a single dashboard. You can schedule posts, track engagement, and monitor conversations. Hootsuite also provides analytics to help you measure the success of your social media efforts.

Another tool that is worth considering is Buffer. It is a social media scheduling tool that allows you to schedule posts across different platforms. You can also track the performance of your posts and optimize your content to improve engagement.

For those who want to monitor their social media mentions and brand reputation, Mention is the perfect tool. It allows you to monitor keywords, hashtags, and social media accounts in real-time. You can also respond to mentions and track the performance of your social media campaigns.

Canva is a graphic design tool that is perfect for creating social media graphics. It has a wide range of templates that you can customize to create stunning visuals for your social media posts. You can also use Canva to create infographics, presentations, and marketing materials.

When it comes to resources, Social Media Examiner is a great website that offers tips, advice, and insights into social media marketing. It covers topics such as Facebook, Instagram, LinkedIn, and Twitter. The website also offers a free newsletter that you can subscribe to for regular updates.

In conclusion, social media management is an essential aspect of any virtual assistant business. By using the right tools and resources, you can manage social media effectively and help your clients achieve their goals.

Email Marketing Services for Virtual Assistant Businesses

The Ultimate Guide to Starting Your Own Virtual Assistant Business

The benefits of email marketing for virtual assistant businesses

As a virtual assistant business owner, you're always looking for effective ways to reach potential clients and grow your business. One powerful tool that you should consider using is email marketing. Email marketing offers numerous benefits for virtual assistant businesses, and in this subchapter, we'll explore some of the most important ones.

First and foremost, email marketing is an incredibly cost-effective way to reach your target audience. Unlike other forms of marketing, such as print or radio ads, email marketing requires very little investment. All you need is an email list and a reliable email marketing platform, and you can start sending out targeted messages to potential clients.

Another major benefit of email marketing is that it allows you to build relationships with your audience. By sending regular emails with helpful tips, industry news, and other relevant content, you can position yourself as an authority in your field and establish trust with potential clients. This can lead to increased business and referrals over time.

Email marketing also gives you the ability to track your results and make data-driven decisions. With most email marketing platforms, you can see exactly how many people open your emails, click on your links, and take other actions. This allows you to refine your messaging and targeting over time to achieve even better results.

Finally, email marketing is extremely flexible and customizable. You can use it to promote a wide range of services, from social media management to website design to administrative support. You can also tailor your messaging to different segments of your email list based on their interests and needs.

In conclusion, email marketing is a powerful tool for any virtual assistant business looking to grow and succeed. By taking advantage of its cost-effectiveness, relationship-building capabilities, data-driven insights, and flexibility, you can reach new audiences and build lasting relationships with potential clients.

How to create successful email campaigns for your clients

Email marketing is a powerful tool that can help you grow your virtual assistant business and provide valuable services to your clients. By creating successful email campaigns, you can help your clients reach their audience, increase their sales, and build strong relationships with their customers.

To create successful email campaigns for your clients, you need to follow a few key steps:

1. Understand your client's audience: The first step is to understand your client's target audience. Learn about their demographic, interests, and behaviors. This will help you create email campaigns that resonate with them and get their attention.

2. Define your client's goals: Before you start creating email campaigns, you need to define your client's goals. Are they trying to promote a new product, increase sales, or build brand awareness? Once you know their goals, you can create email campaigns that align with them.

3. Create engaging content: The content of your email campaigns is key to their success. Your content should be engaging, informative, and relevant to your client's audience. Use catchy subject lines, clear calls to action, and visual elements to make your emails stand out.

4. Optimize for mobile: More than half of all emails are opened on mobile devices. To ensure that your email campaigns are effective, you need to optimize them for mobile. Use responsive design, make your fonts legible, and keep your content concise.

5. Test and analyze: Once you've created your email campaigns, it's important to test and analyze their performance. Use A/B testing to compare different versions of your emails and see which ones perform better. Use analytics tools to track open rates, click-through rates, and conversion rates.

By following these steps, you can create successful email campaigns for your clients and help them achieve their goals. As a virtual assistant, offering email marketing services can be a valuable addition to your list of services and help you stand out from the competition.

How to manage email lists and subscribers

One of the key aspects of running a successful virtual assistant business is managing your email lists and subscribers. In today's digital age, email marketing is a powerful tool for businesses to communicate with their customers and potential clients. However, managing a large email list can be a daunting task. In this subchapter, we will cover some tips on how to effectively manage your email lists and subscribers.

1. Choose the right email marketing service

There are several email marketing services available in the market, each with their own unique features and pricing plans. Before choosing an email marketing service, make sure to research and compare different options to find the one that best suits your business needs. Some popular email marketing services for virtual assistant businesses include Mailchimp, Constant Contact, and ConvertKit.

2. Segment your email list

Segmenting your email list involves dividing your subscribers into smaller groups based on their interests, behaviors, or demographics. This allows you to send targeted and personalized emails to each group, increasing the chances of engagement and conversions. For example, if you offer website design and development services, you can segment your email list into groups such as small businesses, bloggers, and e-commerce stores.

3. Regularly clean your email list

Over time, your email list may accumulate inactive or invalid email addresses, which can negatively impact your email deliverability and open rates. It's important to regularly clean your email list by removing inactive subscribers and fixing any invalid email addresses. This not only improves your email performance but also saves you money on email marketing services.

4. Provide value to your subscribers

Your subscribers have opted-in to your email list because they are interested in your business and what you have to offer. It's important to provide them with valuable content and information in your emails, such as industry insights, tips, and exclusive offers. This not only helps to build trust and loyalty with your subscribers but also increases the chances of them becoming paying clients.

In conclusion, managing your email lists and subscribers is a crucial aspect of running a successful virtual assistant business. By choosing the right email marketing service, segmenting your email list, regularly cleaning your list, and providing value to your subscribers, you can effectively communicate with your target audience and grow your business.

Tools and resources for email marketing

Email marketing has become a crucial tool for businesses looking to connect with their audience and drive conversions. As a virtual assistant, it is essential to have a solid understanding of email marketing and the tools and resources available to help you create effective campaigns. In this subchapter, we will explore some of the best tools and resources for email marketing that can help you grow your virtual assistant business.

One of the most popular email marketing tools is Mailchimp. This platform offers a range of features, including email automation, audience management, and analytics. Mailchimp is free for up to 2,000 subscribers and 10,000 emails per month, making it an affordable option for small businesses. Additionally, Mailchimp offers a range of templates and design tools to help you create stunning emails that engage your audience.

Another popular email marketing tool is Constant Contact. This platform offers similar features to Mailchimp, including automation and analytics. However, Constant Contact also offers social media integration, allowing you to share your emails on your social media channels. Constant Contact also offers a range of customizable templates and design tools, making it easy to create professional-looking emails.

If you are looking for a more comprehensive email marketing solution, you may want to consider HubSpot. This platform offers email marketing, as well as CRM, marketing automation, and sales tools. While HubSpot can be more expensive than other email marketing tools, it offers a range of powerful features that can help you streamline your marketing efforts.

In addition to these email marketing tools, there are also a range of resources available to help you improve your email marketing skills. For example, the HubSpot Academy offers a range of free courses on email marketing, covering topics such as email design, list segmentation, and automation. Additionally, websites such as Email on Acid and Litmus offer tools and resources for testing and optimizing your emails for different devices and email clients.

Overall, email marketing is a critical tool for virtual assistant businesses looking to connect with their audience and drive conversions. By using the right tools and resources, you can create effective email campaigns that help you grow your business and achieve your goals.

Website Design and Development for Virtual Assistant Businesses

The importance of a professional website for virtual assistant businesses

In today's digital age, having a professional website has become a necessity for businesses of all sizes. A website is the virtual storefront of your business, and just like a physical storefront, it should be welcoming, informative and professional. As a virtual assistant, your website is your primary marketing tool, and it is essential that it reflects your brand and services accurately.

A professional website is critical for virtual assistant businesses because it establishes credibility and trust with potential clients. A well-designed website provides a positive first impression and gives the impression that you are a legitimate business. It helps to convey your professionalism, experience and expertise in the industry you are operating in.

Furthermore, a professional website is crucial for showcasing your services and skills. As a virtual assistant, your website should highlight your areas of expertise, such as social media management, administrative support, email marketing, content creation and copywriting. By doing so, potential clients can easily understand your capabilities and decide if your services are what they need.

A professional website is also an excellent tool for lead generation and marketing. With a well-designed website, you can attract potential clients through search engines, social media, and other digital marketing channels. It allows you to showcase your work, testimonials and case studies, and build trust with your audience.

Moreover, a professional website can help streamline your business processes. By integrating your website with tools such as project management systems, invoicing, and scheduling software, you can efficiently manage your workload and provide a better experience for your clients.

In conclusion, a professional website is a crucial component of any virtual assistant business. It establishes credibility, showcases your services and skills, and helps you generate leads and streamline your business. If you are starting your own virtual assistant business, investing in a professional website is a must to succeed in today's competitive digital landscape.

How to design and develop websites for your clients

As a virtual assistant, offering website design and development services can be a lucrative niche to explore. Many businesses, both large and small, require a website to establish their online presence and attract more customers. If you have a knack for design and a grasp of coding languages, you can offer website design and development services to your clients. Here are some steps to follow when designing and developing websites for your clients.

1. Understand Your Client's Needs

Before you start designing a website, you need to understand your client's needs. Talk to your client and ask them what they want to achieve with their website. Do they want to sell products online, showcase their services, or build an online community? Understanding your client's needs will help you design a website that meets their expectations.

2. Choose a Platform

There are several platforms you can use to design and develop websites. Some popular platforms include WordPress, Wix, and Squarespace. Choose a platform that best suits your client's needs and your skill set.

3. Choose a Template or Theme

Once you have chosen a platform, you can choose a template or theme to use for your client's website. Most platforms have pre-designed templates and themes that you can customize to meet your client's needs.

4. Create Content

Once you have chosen a template or theme, it's time to create content for your client's website. This includes writing copy, creating images, and designing graphics. Make sure the content is engaging and informative to attract visitors to the website.

5. Test the Website

Before launching the website, test it to ensure it's functioning properly. Check for broken links, slow loading times, and any other issues that may affect the user experience.

6. Launch the Website

Once you have tested the website and made any necessary changes, it's time to launch it. Make sure your client is happy with the final product before making it live.

In conclusion, website design and development is a valuable niche for virtual assistants. By following these steps, you can design and develop websites that meet your clients' needs and help them establish a strong online presence.

How to manage website maintenance for your clients

As a virtual assistant, one of the services you might offer your clients is website maintenance. This could include updating content, fixing broken links, and ensuring the site is secure and up-to-date. Here are some tips for managing website maintenance for your clients:

1. Set clear expectations: Before you start working with a client, make sure you both have a clear understanding of what website maintenance services you will be providing. This might include how often you will be updating the site, what kinds of updates you will be making, and how you will communicate with the client about any issues or concerns.

2. Use a project management tool: To keep track of website maintenance tasks and deadlines, consider using a project management tool like Trello or Asana. You can create a board or project for each client and use it to track tasks, deadlines, and communication with the client.

3. Keep backups: It's important to keep regular backups of your client's website in case anything goes wrong. This could include backing up the site files, as well as any databases or other data associated with the site. Make sure you have a reliable backup system in place and test it regularly to ensure it's working properly.

4. Stay up-to-date with security: Website security is an important aspect of maintenance, so make sure you stay up-to-date with the latest security threats and vulnerabilities. This might include installing security updates, using strong passwords, and keeping an eye out for any suspicious activity on the site.

5. Communicate regularly with the client: It's important to keep the client informed about any updates or changes you make to their website. This might include sending regular reports or updates, as well as responding promptly to any questions or concerns the client has.

By following these tips, you can provide effective website maintenance services to your clients and help keep their websites running smoothly and securely.

Tools and resources for website design and development

Tools and resources for website design and development

In today's digital age, having a website for your virtual assistant business is crucial. It serves as the face of your business and allows potential clients to learn more about your services, pricing, and contact information. However, designing and developing a website can be a daunting task, especially if you have no prior experience.

Thankfully, there are numerous tools and resources available that make website design and development a breeze. Here are some of the most popular ones:

1. WordPress - This is the most popular content management system (CMS) used for website design and development. It is free and user-friendly, with numerous templates and plugins available to customize your website.

2. Wix - This is a website builder that offers hundreds of templates and drag-and-drop features. It is perfect for those who have no coding experience and want to create a professional-looking website.

3. Squarespace - This is a website builder that offers stunning templates and an easy-to-use interface. It is ideal for those who want a clean and modern design for their website.

4. Canva - This is a graphic design tool that allows you to create stunning graphics for your website. It offers a wide range of templates and design elements, making it perfect for those who have no design experience.

5. Google Analytics - This is a free web analytics service that tracks and reports website traffic. It provides valuable insights into the performance of your website and helps you make informed decisions about your online presence.

6. Yoast SEO - This is a plugin for WordPress that helps improve the search engine optimization (SEO) of your website. It analyzes your content and provides suggestions for improving your ranking on search engines like Google.

7. Fiverr - This is a freelance marketplace where you can hire web designers and developers to create a custom website for your business. It is perfect for those who have no time or desire to design and develop their website themselves.

In conclusion, designing and developing a website for your virtual assistant business is essential in today's digital age. With the tools and resources available, it has never been easier to create a professional-looking website that showcases your skills and services. Whether you choose to use a website builder or hire a freelancer, make sure your website is user-friendly, visually appealing, and optimized for search engines.

Administrative Support for Virtual Assistant Businesses

The different types of administrative support you can offer

When starting your own virtual assistant business, it is important to understand the different types of administrative support you can offer to your clients. This will not only help you determine your niche but also give you a better understanding of the services you can provide to your clients. Here are the different types of administrative support you can offer:

1. Email and calendar management - As a virtual assistant, you can help your clients manage their emails and calendar, schedule appointments, and respond to inquiries.

2. Data entry and management - This involves entering and organizing data into spreadsheets, databases, and other software programs.

3. Bookkeeping and accounting - You can offer bookkeeping and accounting services to your clients, including managing invoices, tracking expenses, and preparing financial statements.

4. Customer service - As a virtual assistant, you can provide customer service support to your clients' customers, handling inquiries, complaints, and feedback.

5. Project management - You can offer project management services to your clients, including managing timelines, coordinating tasks, and ensuring deadlines are met.

6. Travel arrangements - You can help your clients plan and book travel arrangements, including flights, accommodations, and transportation.

7. Social media management - You can offer social media management services to your clients, including creating and scheduling posts, monitoring engagement, and analyzing social media metrics.

8. Email marketing - You can help your clients with email marketing campaigns, including creating and sending newsletters, managing email lists, and analyzing email metrics.

9. Website design and development - You can offer website design and development services to your clients, including creating and updating websites, optimizing for SEO, and managing website content.

10. Content creation and copywriting - You can help your clients with content creation and copywriting, including writing blog posts, creating social media content, and developing marketing materials.

By understanding the different types of administrative support you can offer, you can better determine your niche and tailor your services to meet the specific needs of your clients. This will not only help you stand out in the crowded virtual assistant market but also ensure that you are providing high-quality services to your clients.

How to manage calendars and appointments for your clients

As a virtual assistant, managing appointments and calendars for your clients is an essential part of your job. It is crucial to ensure that appointments are scheduled correctly, and important dates are not missed. Here are some tips on how to manage calendars and appointments for your clients:

1. Use a scheduling tool - There are several scheduling tools available that can help you manage appointments and schedules. Some of the popular ones include Calendly, Acuity Scheduling, and Doodle. These tools allow you to create a calendar where clients can book appointments with you. They also offer features such as reminders, time zone conversion, and customization options.

2. Keep a centralized calendar - It is essential to keep a centralized calendar where you can track all your appointments and deadlines. This will help you avoid double bookings and ensure that you don't miss any important dates. Google Calendar is an excellent option for this as it allows you to create multiple calendars and share them with clients.

3. Set clear expectations - It is essential to set clear expectations with your clients regarding how appointments will be scheduled and how they can reschedule or cancel them. Make sure to communicate your availability and preferred method of communication (email, phone, or video call).

4. Follow up - After scheduling an appointment, make sure to follow up with your client to confirm the date, time, and location. This will help avoid any confusion or misunderstandings.

5. Be flexible - As a virtual assistant, you may have clients in different time zones. Make sure to be flexible with your schedule and accommodate clients' time zones as much as possible.

Managing calendars and appointments may seem overwhelming, but with the right tools and organization, it can be a breeze. By following these tips, you can ensure that your clients' schedules run smoothly, and they receive the best possible service from you.

How to manage travel arrangements for your clients

As a Virtual Assistant, one of the most important tasks you'll be responsible for is managing travel arrangements for your clients. This can be a daunting task, especially if you're new to the industry. However, with the right tools and approach, you can excel at managing travel arrangements and impress your clients with your efficiency and attention to detail.

The first step to managing travel arrangements is to understand your client's needs. What is their travel itinerary, and what are their preferences when it comes to flights, accommodation, and transportation? Do they have any special requirements, such as dietary restrictions or mobility issues? Once you have a clear understanding of their needs, you can begin to research and book their travel arrangements.

When it comes to booking flights, there are a few things to keep in mind. Firstly, try to book flights well in advance to secure the best deals and availability. Secondly, consider using flight comparison websites to compare prices and find the best deals. Finally, be aware of any airline policies or restrictions that may impact your client's travel plans, such as baggage allowances or visa requirements.

Accommodation is another important aspect of travel arrangements. Consider your client's preferences when it comes to location, amenities, and budget. Use websites like Booking.com or Airbnb to find the best options and read reviews from other travelers. Be sure to confirm all reservation details and check-in procedures to avoid any issues upon arrival.

Transportation is also an important consideration when managing travel arrangements. Research the best options for getting around, whether it's public transportation, taxi services, or rental cars. Be sure to arrange transportation to and from the airport and any other destinations on your client's itinerary.

Finally, communication is key when managing travel arrangements. Keep your client updated on the status of their travel plans and any changes that may occur. Be available to answer any questions or concerns they may have, and provide them with all necessary travel documents and information.

In conclusion, managing travel arrangements for your clients requires attention to detail, organization, and effective communication. By understanding your client's needs, researching the best options, and communicating effectively, you can provide excellent service and exceed their expectations.

Tools and resources for administrative support

As a virtual assistant, you need to have the right tools and resources to be able to provide excellent administrative support to your clients. With the right tools, you can streamline your workflow, save time and improve your productivity. Here are some essential tools and resources you need to run a successful virtual assistant business.

1. Project Management Tools: As a virtual assistant, you will be working with clients from different parts of the world, and you need to have a project management tool to keep track of your tasks and deadlines. With tools like Asana, Trello, or Monday.com, you can keep track of your to-do list, assign tasks, and collaborate with your clients.

2. Social Media Tools: Social media management is an essential part of virtual assistant businesses. You need to have the right tools to schedule posts, manage social media accounts, and analyze analytics. Hootsuite, Buffer, and Sprout Social are some of the popular social media management tools you can use.

3. Email Marketing Tools: Email marketing is another essential service offered by virtual assistants. You need email marketing tools like Mailchimp, ConvertKit, or Aweber to create email campaigns, automate your email marketing, and track your email campaigns' performance.

4. Website Design and Development Tools: Website design and development are essential services offered by virtual assistants. You need to have website design tools like WordPress, Wix, or Squarespace to create beautiful and functional websites for your clients.

5. Administrative Tools: Administrative tasks like invoicing, time tracking, and bookkeeping are essential to a virtual assistant business's success. You can use tools like Quickbooks, Freshbooks, or Wave to handle these tasks efficiently.

6. Content Creation Tools: Content creation is another service offered by virtual assistants. You need to have content creation tools like Canva, Adobe Creative Cloud, or Grammarly to create engaging and high-quality content for your clients.

In conclusion, having the right tools and resources is essential to run a successful virtual assistant business. With these tools, you can streamline your workflow, save time, and provide excellent administrative support to your clients.

Content Creation and Copywriting for Virtual Assistant Businesses

The importance of quality content for virtual assistant businesses

One of the most important aspects of running a successful virtual assistant business is producing quality content. Whether you're offering social media management, email marketing services, website design and development, administrative support, or content creation and copywriting, the quality of your work will directly impact your success.

Quality content is essential for establishing credibility and building trust with clients. When potential clients are searching for a virtual assistant, they want to see examples of your work and know that you can deliver results. By producing high-quality content, you demonstrate your expertise and show that you can provide value to your clients.

In addition, quality content is essential for attracting and retaining clients. When clients see the value you provide through your content, they are more likely to become repeat customers and refer you to others. This can lead to a steady stream of business and help you grow your virtual assistant business over time.

When it comes to content creation for virtual assistant businesses, there are a few key things to keep in mind. First, it's important to tailor your content to your target audience. Understanding their needs and pain points will help you create content that resonates with them and provides value.

Second, consistency is key. Whether you're producing blog posts, social media content, or email newsletters, it's important to stick to a regular schedule and deliver high-quality content on a consistent basis. This helps build trust with your audience and ensures that they keep coming back for more.

Finally, it's important to stay up-to-date with the latest trends and best practices in your niche. This will help you stay competitive and provide the best possible service to your clients. Whether that means attending industry conferences, reading industry publications, or taking courses, investing in your own education and development is essential for producing quality content.

In conclusion, quality content is essential for virtual assistant businesses. By producing high-quality content that resonates with your target audience, you can establish credibility, attract and retain clients, and grow your business over time. So if you're looking to start your own virtual assistant business, make sure to prioritize quality content as a key part of your strategy.

How to create content for your clients' blogs and websites

Content creation and copywriting are two critical skills that virtual assistants (VA) need to master if they want to succeed in the online business world. As a VA, one of your primary responsibilities is to create engaging and informative content for your clients' blogs and websites. This content should be designed to attract and retain the attention of their target audience, while also providing value and building trust and credibility for the brand.

Here are some tips on how to create content for your clients' blogs and websites:

1. Know your client's target audience: Before you start creating content, it's essential to understand who your client's target audience is. This will help you tailor your content to their needs and preferences, and ensure that it resonates with them.

2. Research your topic: Conduct thorough research on the topic you're writing about. This will help you create content that is accurate, informative, and up-to-date. Use reliable sources and be sure to double-check your facts before publishing.

3. Write in an engaging and conversational tone: Your content should be easy to read and understand. Use simple language, short sentences, and a conversational tone to make it more engaging and relatable. Avoid using jargon or technical terms that your audience may not be familiar with.

4. Use visuals: Visuals like images, videos, and infographics can help break up long blocks of text and make your content more visually appealing. They can also help illustrate your points and make your content more memorable.

5. Edit and proofread: Always edit and proofread your content before submitting it to your client. Check for spelling and grammar errors, and ensure that your content flows smoothly and logically.

By following these tips, you can create high-quality content that will help your clients attract and retain their target audience. Remember to stay up-to-date with the latest trends and best practices in content creation and copywriting to stay ahead of the competition.

How to write copy for your clients' marketing materials

As a virtual assistant, you will likely be tasked with writing copy for your clients' marketing materials. Whether it's creating content for social media, crafting email marketing campaigns, or developing website copy, it's essential that you understand how to write effective copy that will drive results for your clients.

One of the first steps in writing copy for your clients is to understand their target audience. Who are they trying to reach, and what are their pain points? By understanding their audience, you can tailor your language and messaging to resonate with them and ultimately drive more conversions.

Next, it's important to focus on the benefits of your clients' products or services. Rather than simply listing features, highlight how their offerings will improve their customers' lives or solve a problem they're facing. This approach is much more persuasive and can help your clients stand out from their competitors.

When it comes to social media, it's important to keep your content short and sweet. Social media users have short attention spans, so focus on creating attention-grabbing headlines and engaging visuals. Use language that is conversational and easy to understand, and always include a call to action to encourage your audience to engage with your clients' brand.

Email marketing campaigns require a slightly different approach. Craft subject lines that are attention-grabbing and use language that is personalized and relevant to your audience. Keep your content short and focused, and always include a clear call to action. It's also important to segment your email list so that you can tailor your messaging to specific groups of subscribers.

Website copy should be clear, concise, and focused on the benefits your clients' products or services provide. Use headlines and subheadings to break up content and make it easy to scan, and be sure to include clear calls to action throughout the site.

Ultimately, the key to writing effective copy for your clients is to understand their audience, focus on benefits over features, and tailor your language and messaging to resonate with them. By doing so, you can help your clients achieve their marketing goals and drive real results for their business.

Tools and resources for content creation and copywriting

Content creation and copywriting are critical components of any virtual assistant business. They are the lifeblood of any successful online presence. In order to create effective content and copy, you need the right tools and resources. Here are some of the tools and resources that can help you create high-quality content and copy for your virtual assistant business.

Firstly, you need to have a strong understanding of your target audience. This will help you tailor your content and copy to their needs and preferences. Social media platforms like Facebook, Twitter, and LinkedIn can be a great resource for gathering information about your target audience. You can also use tools like Google Analytics to track the behavior of your website visitors and see what content and copy resonates with them.

In addition to understanding your target audience, you need to have a solid grasp of the principles of good copywriting. There are many resources available online that can help you learn the basics of copywriting, such as the Copyblogger blog and the book "The Elements of Style" by William Strunk Jr. and E.B. White.

Once you have a good understanding of your target audience and the principles of good copywriting, you need to have the right tools to create and publish content. Some of the essential tools for content creation and copywriting include a word processor like Microsoft Word or Google Docs, a grammar checker like Grammarly, and a content management system like WordPress.

Finally, you need to have a system in place for managing and organizing your content. This includes tools for scheduling and publishing content, as well as tools for tracking and measuring the performance of your content. Some of the best tools for content management and organization include Hootsuite, Buffer, and Google Analytics.

In conclusion, content creation and copywriting are critical components of any virtual assistant business. By understanding your target audience, learning the principles of good copywriting, and using the right tools and resources, you can create high-quality content and copy that will help your business succeed.

Growing Your Virtual Assistant Business

How to get more clients for your virtual assistant business

As a virtual assistant business owner, one of the most important aspects of your success is getting more clients. The more clients you have, the more income you can generate and the more you can grow your business. Here are some effective tips on how to get more clients for your virtual assistant business:

1. Define your niche and target market: To attract clients, it is important to specialize in a particular niche or industry. Determine what services you offer best and what industries you have the most experience in. This will help you identify your target market and tailor your marketing efforts to attract the right clients.

2. Leverage social media: Social media platforms such as LinkedIn, Twitter, and Facebook are great tools to connect with potential clients. Use these platforms to showcase your skills and expertise, share valuable content, and engage with your target audience. Social media also allows you to network with other virtual assistants and industry professionals.

3. Offer free trials or consultations: Offering free trials or consultations is a great way to showcase your skills and demonstrate the value you can bring to a client's business. This can help potential clients feel more comfortable and confident in your abilities before making a commitment.

4. Utilize email marketing: Email marketing is a powerful tool for virtual assistant businesses. Build an email list of potential clients and regularly send out newsletters or promotional emails to keep them engaged and informed about your services.

5. Create a professional website: A professional website is essential for any virtual assistant business. It should showcase your services, skills, and experience, and make it easy for potential clients to contact you. Ensure your website is mobile-friendly, easy to navigate, and has engaging content.

6. Build a strong portfolio: A portfolio is a great way to showcase your skills and experience to potential clients. Include case studies, testimonials, and examples of your work to demonstrate your expertise.

7. Network with other professionals: Networking with other virtual assistants and industry professionals can help you build relationships and generate referrals. Attend industry events and conferences, join online forums, and participate in social media groups to connect with others in the industry.

By implementing these tips, you can attract more clients and grow your virtual assistant business. Remember to focus on providing high-quality services and building strong relationships with your clients to ensure long-term success.

How to manage your workload and time effectively

One of the biggest challenges faced by virtual assistants (VA) is managing their workload and time effectively. With so many tasks to complete and deadlines to meet, it's easy to get overwhelmed and stressed out. However, with the right strategies and tools in place, you can improve your productivity and achieve your goals.

Here are some tips on how to manage your workload and time effectively as a virtual assistant:

1. Prioritize your tasks: Make a list of all the tasks you need to do and prioritize them based on their importance and urgency. Focus on completing the most important tasks first, and then move on to the less important ones.

2. Use a calendar: Use a calendar to schedule your tasks and deadlines. This will help you stay organized and ensure that you don't miss any deadlines.

3. Set realistic goals: Set realistic goals for yourself and break them down into smaller, manageable tasks. This will help you stay motivated and on track.

4. Use time-tracking tools: Use time-tracking tools to track how much time you spend on each task. This will help you identify areas where you can improve your productivity.

5. Take breaks: Take regular breaks throughout the day to avoid burnout. Use this time to recharge your batteries and come back to your work with renewed energy and focus.

6. Outsource tasks: Consider outsourcing tasks that are not your core strengths or that take up too much of your time. This will free up your time to focus on the tasks that you are best at and that generate the most revenue for your business.

7. Automate tasks: Use automation tools to automate tasks such as email marketing, social media management, and website maintenance. This will save you time and help you focus on more important tasks.

By implementing these strategies, you can manage your workload and time effectively as a virtual assistant. This will help you achieve your goals and grow your business.

How to scale your virtual assistant business for growth

If you're a virtual assistant who has been in the industry for a few years, you may be wondering how to scale your business for growth. Scaling your virtual assistant business is important for a number of reasons, including increasing your income, expanding your client base, and reducing the amount of time you have to spend on administrative tasks.

Here are some tips for scaling your virtual assistant business for growth:

1. Specialize in a niche

One of the best ways to scale your virtual assistant business is to specialize in a niche. By focusing on a specific area, such as social media management or email marketing services, you can become an expert in that field and attract more clients who need those services.

2. Hire other virtual assistants

As your business grows, you may find that you have more work than you can handle on your own. In this case, you can hire other virtual assistants to help you with the workload. This will allow you to take on more clients and projects, and increase your income.

3. Offer website design and development services

Many businesses need help with website design and development, so offering these services can help you attract more clients. You can either learn how to do website design and development yourself, or outsource this work to a freelancer.

4. Provide administrative support

Administrative support is a common service that virtual assistants offer, but it's also a service that can be scaled for growth. By offering administrative support to businesses in a specific industry, such as healthcare or finance, you can become an expert in that field and attract more clients.

5. Create content for your clients

Content creation and copywriting are important services that many businesses need. By offering these services, you can help your clients attract more customers and grow their businesses. You can also create content for your own website or blog, which can help attract more potential clients.

In conclusion, scaling your virtual assistant business for growth is an important step in increasing your income and expanding your client base. By specializing in a niche, hiring other virtual assistants, offering website design and development services, providing administrative support, and creating content for your clients, you can take your virtual assistant business to the next level.

Tips for success as a virtual assistant business owner

Tips for success as a virtual assistant business owner

Starting your own virtual assistant business can be an exciting and rewarding experience. However, it can also be challenging, especially if you don't know where to start or how to grow your business. Here are some tips to help you succeed as a virtual assistant business owner.

1. Define your niche

One of the most important things you can do when starting a virtual assistant business is to define your niche. There are many different niches within the virtual assistant industry, including social media management, email marketing, website design and development, administrative support, and content creation. By identifying your niche, you can focus your marketing efforts and attract clients who are looking for the services you offer.

2. Develop a business plan

A business plan is essential for any business, including a virtual assistant business. Your business plan should include your goals, target market, services, pricing, marketing strategies, and financial projections. It will serve as a roadmap for your business, helping you stay on track and measure your progress.

3. Build a strong online presence

As a virtual assistant, your online presence is crucial. You need to have a professional website that showcases your services, testimonials from satisfied clients, and a portfolio of your work. You should also have a presence on social media platforms, such as LinkedIn and Twitter, where you can connect with potential clients and showcase your expertise.

4. Provide excellent customer service

In the virtual assistant industry, word-of-mouth referrals are essential. To grow your business, you need to provide excellent customer service to your clients. This means responding to emails and phone calls promptly, delivering high-quality work on time, and going above and beyond to exceed your clients' expectations.

5. Continuously learn and improve

To stay competitive in the virtual assistant industry, you need to continuously learn and improve your skills. Attend webinars, read industry blogs, and invest in training courses to stay up-to-date on the latest trends and best practices in your niche. By continuously improving your skills, you can offer more value to your clients and grow your business.

In conclusion, starting a virtual assistant business can be a lucrative and fulfilling career choice. By following these tips, you can set yourself up for success and build a thriving business that meets the needs of your clients.

Conclusion

The benefits of starting a virtual assistant business

The Benefits of Starting a Virtual Assistant Business

Starting a virtual assistant business can be a great way to earn a living while working from home. Here are some of the benefits of starting your own virtual assistant business:

Flexibility

One of the biggest benefits of starting a virtual assistant business is the flexibility it provides. You can work from anywhere at any time, as long as you have an internet connection. This means you can work around your schedule and other commitments, such as caring for children or elderly parents.

Low start-up costs

Starting a virtual assistant business requires very little start-up capital. You don't need to rent an office space, purchase expensive equipment or hire staff. All you need is a computer, internet connection, and some software tools.

High demand

As more businesses move online, the demand for virtual assistants is growing. Many businesses are looking for affordable ways to outsource administrative tasks, social media management, email marketing, website design, content creation, and copywriting. This means that there is a high demand for virtual assistants who can provide these services.

Variety of niches

There are many niches within the virtual assistant industry, so you can choose to specialize in a particular area, such as social media management, email marketing, website design, administrative support, content creation, or copywriting. This means you can cater to the specific needs of your clients and create a niche for yourself.

Opportunity to work with a variety of clients

Starting a virtual assistant business allows you to work with a variety of clients from different industries. This means you can learn about different businesses and industries, which can be both interesting and educational.

Increased earning potential

As your virtual assistant business grows, you can increase your earning potential. You can charge more for your services, take on more clients, and expand your business to include additional services.

In conclusion, starting a virtual assistant business can be a great way to earn a living while working from home. It provides flexibility, low start-up costs, high demand, a variety of niches, the opportunity to work with a variety of clients, and increased earning potential. If you're interested in starting your own virtual assistant business, there are many resources available to help you get started.

How this book can help you start and grow your virtual assistant business

Are you interested in starting a virtual assistant business but don't know where to begin? Look no further! This book is the ultimate guide to starting and growing your own virtual assistant business. Whether you're looking for a side hustle or a full-time career, this book has everything you need to know.

Firstly, this book will teach you the basics of starting a virtual assistant business. You'll learn how to identify your niche, set your rates, and find clients. You'll also learn how to create a business plan and set goals for your business.

Once you've got the basics down, this book will teach you how to grow your business. You'll learn how to market your services, build your online presence, and create a strong brand. You'll also learn how to build a team of virtual assistants to help you grow your business.

But that's not all! This book also covers specific niches within the virtual assistant industry. Whether you're interested in social media management, email marketing, website design, administrative support, or content creation, this book has you covered. You'll learn the skills you need to offer these services to your clients and how to market yourself in these niches.

Overall, this book is the ultimate guide to starting and growing your own virtual assistant business. It's perfect for anyone who is interested in starting a side hustle or a full-time career in the virtual assistant industry. With this book, you'll have all the tools you need to succeed and build a thriving virtual assistant business.

Final thoughts and next steps.

Final Thoughts and Next Steps

Congratulations! You have made it to the end of The Ultimate Guide to Starting Your Own Virtual Assistant Business. By now, you should have a solid understanding of what it takes to start and grow a successful virtual assistant business. As you embark on this journey, remember that there will be ups and downs, but with hard work and dedication, you can achieve your goals.

It is essential to keep in mind that your success as a virtual assistant will depend on your ability to provide excellent service to your clients consistently. You will need to be organized, detail-oriented, and able to manage your time effectively. Additionally, you will need to stay up-to-date with the latest industry trends and technology to remain competitive.

As you begin your journey, it is crucial to identify your niche. Whether you choose to specialize in social media management, email marketing services, website design and development, administrative support, or content creation and copywriting, ensure that you have the necessary skills and experience to provide exceptional service to your clients.

Next, you need to create a business plan. A well-defined business plan will help you establish your objectives, identify your target market, and develop a marketing strategy to grow your business. Don't forget to factor in your pricing structure, expenses, and revenue projections to ensure that your business is profitable.

As you start your business, it is essential to market yourself effectively. Utilize social media platforms, networking events, and online directories to promote your services and build your brand. Additionally, prioritize building relationships with potential clients and delivering exceptional service to ensure repeat business and referrals.

In conclusion, starting a virtual assistant business can be a fulfilling and profitable venture. With the right mindset, skills, and resources, you can turn your passion for helping others into a successful career. Remember to stay focused, continue learning, and always put your clients first. Good luck on your journey!

The Ultimate Guide to Starting Your Own Virtual Assistant Business

Best of luck! Your virtual assistant journey starts now.

Neil King